HOOD COUNTY PUBLIC LIBRARY
105162

AF580286

Taking punishment from Joe Frazier, right, Muhammad Ali snapped back to win a unanimous decision in this January, 1974, bout. It was another step in his long road back to the heavyweight championship.

SPORTS CLASSIC

BOXING'S HEAVYWEIGHT CHAMPIONSHIP FIGHT

By JULIAN MAY

Creative Education
Childrens Press

PHOTO CREDITS:

UPI . . . . Cover, 2, 8, 11, 14, 17, 19, 20, 22, 27, 29, 31, 33, 35, 37, 38, 41, 42, 46
Wide World 1, 25, 45

Published by Creative Educational Society, Inc., 123 South Broad Street, Mankato, Minnesota 56001. Printed in the United States.

Library of Congress Cataloging in Publication Data
May, Julian.
Boxing's heavyweight championship.
(Sports classic)
SUMMARY: Discusses boxing in the United States and some of the heavyweight champions of the world.
1. Boxing—History—Juvenile literature. [1. Boxing—History. 2. Boxing—Biography] I. Title.
GV1121.M39 796.8'3'0922 [B] 76-4861 ISBN 0-87191-503-0

Contents

Boxing's Golden Age

Man versus man. The only weapons, doubled-up fists. A contest so basic, so primitive, that it must have its origins in cave-man days.

This is boxing. It has been called brutal, cruel, degrading. It has been praised as a demonstration of manly courage and physical skill. It has been forbidden by law in English-speaking lands. As late as 1900, it was banned in most of the United States.

But boxing flourished, even when it had to go underground. It appealed not only to the uneducated, but also to men of culture and learning — and to women, too. Humanitarians have denounced it. Philosophers have condemned it. But there is something about human beings that enjoys a good fight!

Prize fighting in the American colonies seems to have begun in the South. Wealthy planters who had watched prize fights in England came home and trained black slaves to box. The very first man to be called "champion of America" was Tom Molineaux, a slave who won his freedom early in the 1800's by knocking out a rival black boxer.

Early contests, usually fought with bare knuckles, permitted wrestling and all kinds of dirty tactics. In 1865, however, England's Marquis of

The first American heavyweight title fight under the Marquis of Queensbury Rules pitted "Gentleman Jim" Corbett against John L. Sullivan. Corbett won.

Queensbury devised a new set of rules that gave us the modern-day form of boxing. Queensbury rules called for a ring, for the use of gloves, and for 3-minute rounds. Wrestling was forbidden, and a contestant could not be hit if he went down on one knee. If a man was knocked down, he was allowed 10 seconds to rise or else be declared loser by a knockout.

Queensbury rules were not widely adopted for many years in America. As a result, most fights were either brutal blood baths or dishonest "fixes." It was small wonder that boxing was illegal in every state.

One man changed boxing's bad image. He was John L. Sullivan, the first man to be acknowledged in record books as "heavyweight champion."

Sullivan was the son of Irish immigrants. He gloried in the fact that his bouts were always "on the level." He began boxing in 1877. Using both gloves and bare fists, he knocked out every man who opposed him in the ring.

On February 7, 1882, Sullivan met Paddy Ryan for the American championship. The great fight took place at a resort in Mississippi City, Miss., safe from the prying eyes of the law. Using bare knuckles, the Great John L. knocked out Ryan in the ninth round.

Sullivan held his title for 10 years and probably KO'ed at least 200 opponents. One of his most famous fights was against Jake Kilrain on July 8, 1889. Kilrain had been proclaimed heavyweight champ of the world after conquering an English boxer.

The fight stretched out for 75 rounds with the temperature hovering over 100 degrees. At the end, Kilrain was such a wreck that his seconds threw in the sponge, conceding defeat. John L. was still strong and fit, the undisputed heavyweight champion of the world.

This fight was the last championship bout to be fought with bare knuckles. Sullivan became a great celebrity, and slowly boxing emerged from the shadows and became a legitimate sport.

The 1890's saw the rise of three master boxers, so talented that they created a Golden Age of the prize ring. "Gentleman Jim" Corbett defeated John L. Sullivan and became heavyweight champ in 1892, knocking out his opponent in the 21st round.

Corbett held onto the title until 1897. At that time he met a lanky, freckled New Zealander named Bob Fitzsimmons. The match was held in Carson City, Nevada; and both Bat Masterson and Wyatt Earp were on hand to keep the peace. Corbett, famed for his footwork, peppered Fitzsimmons with blows during the early rounds and seemed to have the advantage.

The stolid New Zealander just seemed to stand there and take it. He was waiting, and in the 13th round he struck. One pile-driver fist struck Corbett in the solar plexus; another caught the champ in the jaw. Corbett went down, and Fitzsimmons was heavyweight champion of the world.

Fitzsimmons did not defend his title again until 1899. At that time he took on Jim Jeffries, a huge American with ham-sized fists and a crouch that made him difficult to hit. Jeffries was 13 years younger than the defending champion and 50 pounds heavier, but he was a 3-to-1 underdog in the fight.

Massive Jim Jeffries, right, defends his title against former champ Jim Corbett.

In the fifth round, Fitz landed his deadly solar plexus punch. Jeffries refused to topple! One of the strongest men ever to enter the ring, he was immune to the old champ's blows. Fitzsimmons began to tire under Jeffries' pummeling. In the 11th round, he keeled over for the last time.

"Big Jeff" successfully defended his title again and again. He was never knocked off his feet. Finally, in 1904 he decided to retire from the ring. He himself decided to pick his successor (which he had no right to do) by staging a match between Marvin Hart and Jack Root. Jeffries refereed this fight, which took place on July 3, 1905. Hart won in 12 rounds, but few fight fans accepted him as the legitimate world champion.

Just six months after being crowned by Jeffries, Hart fought Canadian Tommy Burns, whose real name was Noah Brusso. With Jeffries once again officiating, the fight went 20 rounds. Burns won by a decision and was proclaimed the new champion.

But once again there was controversy. The scrappy Canadian had to prove himself by KO'ing eight challengers in a row before he was accepted as the genuine champion of the world.

Black Champion and White Hope

Up until this time, no black man had managed to reach the top ranks in boxing. There were plenty of Negro fighters, but white audiences were not much interested in them. It was a popular myth that black fighters were apt to be cowards in the ring. They were not taken seriously as contenders until the dawn of the 20th century.

Then came Jack Johnson. Many historians of boxing rank him as the best fighter who ever lived. He was born in Galveston, Texas, in 1878, the son of a lay preacher who earned a living as a school janitor. Quick-witted and possessed of a magnificent body, young Jack learned to fight while working as a longshoreman on the docks. He later worked in a gymnasium, where he polished his boxing skill, and prowled restlessly around the country as a hobo.

Jack got his big chance at a carnival in 1897. One of the show attractions was a boxer who challenged members of the audience to fight. Anyone foolish enough to climb into the ring would be herded against a canvas curtain, where a hidden accomplice of the boxer would wallop him over the head with a blackjack.

Young Johnson accepted the challenge and refused to be maneuvered. Using pro-style footwork, Jack met the bruiser with a smile and lightning-fast punches. The hidden blackjacker never got

Smiling as he easily overcomes his hog-fat rival, Jack Johnson pummels Jim Jeffries in the famous "White Hope" match of 1910.

a chance to use his tool. Johnson destroyed his opponent in three rounds.

After this, Johnson was able to become a pro boxer. As the years passed, he slowly built up a reputation and began earning large sums for his matches. Almost all of his opponents were black men; but Johnson was confident he could lick any white fighter, too. He demanded the chance to prove it.

The opportunity finally came in Sydney, Australia, on December 26, 1908. Tommy Burns, the Canadian champion, agreed to meet Johnson. The fight would have bitter racial overtones, with both men publicly reviling one another. But when they were at last glove to glove, it was plain that Johnson was far superior. Smiling and trading curses, Johnson battered the smaller Burns almost playfully. In the 14th round Burns was knocked into a daze, and the police stopped the match. Jack Johnson was declared heavyweight champion of the world by a knockout.

A black man world champion! The boxing world was in a turmoil. A lot of white fans were outraged, not only because of Johnson's race, but also because the new champ was a proud and flashy character who "didn't know his place."

In the years that followed, a number of fighters tried to dethrone Johnson. They were called boxing's White Hopes. Johnson flattened them all.

The pressure grew for Jim Jeffries to come out of retirement and take care of the upstart Negro. Finally he agreed. The match, held in Reno, Nevada, on July 4, 1910, pitted the black champion against the Great White Hope. Jeffries was favored to win; but he was now 35 years old – slow, fat, and out of shape.

Jack Johnson, grinning and invincible, did just as he pleased with Jeffries. In the 15th round, Jim's seconds threw in the sponge.

Other White Hopes met Johnson after that. In trouble with the law, Johnson left the United States and did his fighting in other countries. It was not until he was 37 years old that he met his match. In 1915, in Havana, Cuba, Jack Johnson was defeated by Jess Willard, an ex-ranchhand from Kansas.

Prejudiced boxing fans relaxed. The white race had triumphed, for a while, at least.

Young Jack Dempsey, left, quickly asserts his mastery on Jess Willard.

HR & CO.

Dempsey versus Tunney

Willard, although big and strong, proved to be a "cheese champ" without any real skill. He defended his title only twice. The first time, he dodged through a colorless "no-decision" match. The second time, Willard agreed to meet a young fighter named Jack Dempsey. The encounter took place on July 4, 1919.

The young challenger came from Manassa, Colorado, where he had been a copper miner. He had an impressive record as a fighter and was known for his fiery style. Dempsey stood 6-foot-1 and weighed 191 pounds. Willard was a mountainous 6-foot-6 and weighed 245.

The fight was scheduled for 12 rounds; but just 1 minute and 58 seconds after the opening gong, Willard went down, battered and bleeding. He arose, but the outcome of the fight was plain. Round 1 ended with Willard a pathetic ruin. Dempsey was a ferocious whirlwind, justifying his nickname of Manassa Mauler.

All Willard seemed to do was absorb punishment. The crowd urged the referee to stop the fight at the end of the 2nd round, but Willard insisted on coming back one last time. As the 3rd round gong sounded, Willard had to be dragged to his corner. There he conceded the fight, and Jack Dempsey became heavyweight champion at the age of 24.

In the early 20's, when Dempsey began his reign

An outclassed Willard bows to Dempsey during their duel for the heavyweight championship.

as king of the ring, boxing had at last emerged from its limbo. Regulated by laws, it was now legal in most places. Its popularity swelled. Two of Dempsey's title-defending fights — with Carpentier of France and Firpo of Argentina — had gate receipts of over a million dollars.

In 1926 Dempsey was challenged by Gene Tunney, an up-and-coming fighter who used finesse instead of brute strength. Famed for his defense, Tunney was able to surprise Dempsey in the first moments of their title bout by unleasing a roundhouse right.

Dempsey was stunned and demoralized. After the scheduled ten rounds, the challenger was fresh and spunky; while Dempsey was battered and drooping. Tunney was awarded the championship on a decision.

Dempsey vowed to make a come-back. Less than a year later, on September 22, 1927, a rematch was scheduled. A record-breaking crowd of 100,000 people watched it in Chicago's Soldier Field.

They saw Tunney box expertly and seem to lead in points. But in round eight, Dempsey uncoiled a left hook and flattened the champ. Then, instead of going to a neutral corner, Dempsey stood over Tunney. This delayed the count by four seconds and was enough to save Tunney. He arose at the nine-count, recovered his strength, and won by a decision in ten rounds.

Gene Tunney hits the canvas in the 7th round of the famous bout with Jack Dempsey, held September 22, 1927.

The Brown Bomber

Jack Dempsey retired, and Gene Tunney lacked the magic to draw out huge numbers of fans. As the 1920's drew to a close, boxing's second great Golden Age ended as well.

The early 30's saw the heavyweight crown worn by a collection of second-rate mitt artists — Max Schmeling of Germany, Jack Sharkey, Primo Carnera of Italy, "Madcap Maxie" Baer, and James J. Braddock. When Braddock became champion in 1935, he considered the fact that the previous three champs had held the title only a single year. Braddock didn't want to suffer their shame, so he rested for two years.

Meanwhile, a young black fighter was restoring excitement to the world of boxing. He was Joe Louis Barrow, son of an Alabama sharecropper, owner of the fastest fists in the country. Known professionally as Joe Louis, he was shy before reporters but dynamite in the ring. He slaughtered Primo Carnera, who outweighed him by 60 pounds. He reduced Max Baer to a frightened hulk.

He took on Max Schmeling, full of confidence, widely admired by both blacks and whites. Schmeling, on the other hand, was a citizen of Nazi Germany, whose philosophers said that blacks were an inferior race. In the fight, which took place in

A great contender of the 1920's, Luis Angel Firpo, knocks title-holder Jack Dempsey out of the ring. Firpo, an Argentine, was called the "Wild Bull of the Pampas." He lost this bout to Dempsey.

June, 1936, Joe Louis was out-boxed and out-slugged by Schmeling. He was counted out in the 12th round.

Humiliated, Joe said, "I done everybody wrong." Some sportswriters jeered that the man some had called "Brown Bomber" and "Black Avenger" was only a puffed-up myth. Prejudiced Americans were glad Louis had lost.

Joe Louis knew that he was good; over-confidence, not lack of ability, had done him in. He met ex-champ Jack Sharkey two months later and knocked him out. He waded through the other heavyweight contenders and won every fight.

It was time for a match with Jim Braddock, the sideline-sitting title-holder. On June 22, 1937, Louis and Braddock met at last.

In the first round, the aging champion took the offensive and knocked Joe down with a right to the jaw, but the black contender bounced up again and seemed none the worse. In round 2, Joe took the lead, his youth and quick reflexes giving him the advantage. Braddock began to waver as Joe battered him about the head. By the 7th round, he was so far gone that his seconds wanted to throw in the towel. "You do, and I'll never speak to you again," said Braddock. Game to the end, he was finally floored by Joe Louis' flailing fists and counted out in round 8.

Joe Louis, the Brown Bomber, had become the heavyweight champion of the world. The defeated Braddock said, "Joe has done more to bring boxing

Max Baer cowers as he ducks a Joe Louis right.

back than anyone in the game today. He deserves to be champion."

There were a lot of people who still objected to the notion of a black man owning the heavyweight title. Joe Louis would not be allowed to rest on his laurels as Braddock had. He would be forced to defend his championship, and he was willing.

"I'll be a *fighting* champion," he said.

Joe clobbered several contenders. Then he got a chance to meet his most hated rival, German Max Schmeling. A huge crowd packed Yankee Stadium to watch the bout, held on June 22, 1938. The fight had international political overtones. Roosevelt had encouraged Joe Louis to "beat Germany." Hitler cabled Schmeling wishes for success.

When the two fighters met, Joe attacked with unusual fury. He rained blows on Max's head, jabbed him in the right side, and sent Schmeling to the canvas. The German got up only to be floored three more times by Joe Louis. As the American crowd screamed and cheered, Max Schmeling was counted out after 2 minutes and 4 seconds of the first round.

Joe's victory over Schmeling made him a hero to many Americans. He became one of the best-loved champions and the one who risked his title more than any other. During his 11-year reign (with time out for wartime service) Joe Louis defended his championship 25 times.

In his last title bout, Joe KO'ed Jersey Joe Walcott. He retired undefeated on March 1, 1949.

German Max Schmeling, left, meets Joe Louis in the famous rematch of 1938.

The Comeback of Jersey Joe

Arnold Cream, alias Jersey Joe Walcott, had been born in 1914 and began boxing when he was barely 15 years old. He was determined but not very talented. At the age of 30, he seemed washed up.

Then a new manager, Felix Bocchiccio, took Walcott under his wing. The aging but ring-wise fighter began to rise as a heavyweight contender at a time when most boxers have retired to their rocking chairs. He fought Joe Louis in 1947 and nearly won. After Louis retired, Walcott vied for the vacant title with Ezzard Charles, but lost to the younger man on June 22, 1949.

In 1950, Walcott had another chance at Charles, his fourth try for the heavyweight crown. Jersey Joe was out-classed in 15 rounds. People were sure he was through.

But in 1951, Walcott got still another opportunity at Charles's title. Old Jersey Joe was then 37; the odds against him were 6 to 1. In true storybook fashion, however, after trailing in points throughout 6 rounds, Jersey Joe knocked out the champ with a mighty left hook and became champion of the world.

The "Cinderella Champ" was a great public favorite. He kept his title until September 23, 1952, when he yielded to Rocky Marciano after a valiant 15-round contest.

World heavyweight champ Jersey Joe Walcott, left, compares belts with the lightweight titleholder, Jimmy Carter, in 1951.

Good Guys & Bad Guys

Rocky Marciano was destined to retain his crown for four years, defending it six times against lackluster opponents. He was the only heavyweight champion never to have lost a fight, and 43 of his 49 victories were KO's. He retired with honor in 1956, and his title passed to 21-year-old Floyd Patterson.

During his early boyhood, Patterson was a troublemaker. He was straightened out by a kindly teacher who steered him into boxing. Floyd went to the Olympic Games in 1952 and won the middleweight championship when he was only 17.

Patterson defended his title 5 times, keeping the championship until 1959. At that time he lost in a shocking upset to an unknown Swede, Ingemar Johansson. There was a rematch a year later. This time Patterson knocked his rival cold in the 5th round. He thus became the first ex-champ to regain his title.

Patterson's best years, however, were behind him. In 1962, the handsome, clean-living champ came up against Sonny Liston, an ex-con whose ring career had been guided by hoodlums. Liston was 25 pounds heavier than Patterson and much stronger. The glowering challenger knocked Patterson out in the first round.

Gloom settled over the boxing scene. A "bad guy" was now champion of the world.

In 1959, Floyd Patterson lost his title to Ingemar Johansson of Sweden. It was one of boxing's greatest upsets.

Mighty Mouth Arrives

Sonny Liston tried to live down his bad past. He got rid of his crooked pals and cultivated a wholesome image. In a rematch in 1963, Liston again defeated Patterson. Sportswriters agreed he was a genuine champion, but fans remained cool toward him.

Meanwhile, a more attractive fighter was waiting in the wings. His name was Cassius Marcellus Clay, Jr., and he was destined to become the most controversial black champion since Jack Johnson.

Born in Louisville in 1942, young Clay began boxing at the age of 12 in a boys' club run by a city policeman. Cassius won 6 state Golden Gloves tournaments. In 1959 and 1960, he won both the National Golden Gloves and the National Amateur Athletic Union championships. At the age of 18, he won the gold medal in the light heavyweight division at the Olympic Games.

Just one thing was wrong with this good-looking, talented lad. He had a big mouth.

"I am the greatest!" Cassius would crow. "I am as pretty as a girl! Nobody lays a glove on me!" His bragging made a lot of fans — and a lot of fighters — mad. People wanted to see Cassius Clay get whipped, but he just wouldn't oblige!

After the 1960 Olympics, Clay turned pro. Managed by Angelo Dundee, he did not lose a fight. He

Looming over a fallen opponent, Cassius Clay jeers at his rival. He was famous for making taunts as he fought.

began reciting little poems about his rivals. Before a bout with Archie Moore, Cassius proclaimed:

"When you come to the fight
Don't block aisle or door;
'Cause old Archie Moore
Will fall in four!"

After his prediction about Moore came true, Clay, mouth and all, was finally taken seriously by the boxing world. He fought tough Doug Jones and won a 10-round decision. Then he demanded the right to meet the champion, Sonny Liston.

"I'm faster than Sonny, younger than Sonny, bigger than Sonny, and prettier than Sonny!" the young man bragged. "Sonny Liston is too ugly to be champion!"

The cold-eyed title-holder merely growled, "I don't think the kid's got all his marbles."

When a match was finally arranged, Cassius and his hangers-on turned the weigh-in into a circus. They pranced around, chanting, "Float like a butterfly, sting like a bee!" Cassius pretended to go berserk and tried to attack Liston. He acted like such a clown that most people thought he was scared of the hulking champ. The odds against Clay were 10 to 1.

The fight took place on February 15, 1964. The arena was only half-filled, for most people expected Liston to make short work of the Louisville Lip.

What they saw instead was a fast, expert young boxer who shed his crazy image along with his robe. In the ring, Cassius Clay was all fighter. He destroyed Sonny Liston in 6 rounds. As the gong sounded for the 7th, Liston would not leave his corner. Cassius Clay had won.

"I'm the greatest!" he shouted. "I'm king!"

Cassius Clay, right, meets Sonny Liston for the 1964 championship fight.

EVERLAST
EVERLAST

The Fight of the Century

After winning the world championship, Cassius announced that he had been converted to the Black Muslim religion. This sect, it was said, preached hatred of white people. Cassius also declared that he was taking a new name — Muhammad Ali.

There was a public uproar. A lot of people were afraid that the Black Muslims would start a race war, and here was the heavyweight champ lending his name to the Muslim cause! The Louisville Lip wasn't funny any more.

During the next three years, Muhammad Ali defended his title nine times. He was called a traitor and racist, even though he cheerfully said that he didn't hate anybody.

Then, on April 28, 1967, Ali refused to be inducted into the U.S. Army. He declared that fighting in the Vietnam War violated his religious beliefs. He was indicted for draft evasion, and the World Boxing Association used this as an excuse to strip him of his heavyweight crown. An elimination tournament would decide the new champion.

Before the tournament could be completed, New York State decided to sanction its own world heavyweight fight. On March 4, 1968, Smokin' Joe Frazier defeated Buster Mathis and was declared "champion." A month or so later, Jimmy Ellis was proclaimed to be the title-holder by the WBA. It was a mess.

Joe Frazier drives a hard right to Buster Mathis in the 11th round of their 1968 "title" bout. Later in the round, Frazier won by a knockout.

Joe Frazier is led to a neutral corner after sending Muhammad Ali to the deck during the 15th round of their 1971 fight.

The mess was partially resolved when the rival champs met on February 16, 1970. Joe Frazier won by a TKO in the fifth round. But Muhammad Ali said, "He's nothing but a pretender! I'm the real champ. I have never been defeated!"

Ali's boxing license was finally restored by a court order. He returned to the ring late in 1970 and warmed up by defeating Jerry Quarry and Oscar Bonavena. Then he declared he was ready to meet Joe Frazier.

People called it the "Fight of the Century." Ali was favored to win. He mockingly predicted that Frazier would fall in the 6th round. A huge crowd packed Madison Square Garden on March 8, 1971, to watch the contest.

Frazier was smaller, more plodding, but a fierce slugger of undeniable power. Ali was a graceful dancer with popping blows that wore opponents out. The contenders were well-matched, and the fight was a thrilling one.

At first, Frazier swung at the air as Ali sneered. But in the 4th round, one of Frazier's mighty swings connected with Ali's face. He began to slow. The 6th round came and went, with Frazier still punching; so much for Ali's prediction. As round followed round, Frazier absorbed terrific punishment but kept on slugging. Both men were nearly played out by the end of the 14th round.

As the bell rang for the 15th and last round, Frazier came out smokin' and caught Ali with a mighty left hook. Ali went down. He was able to get up, but the referees decreed that Joe Frazier had won the "Fight of the Century" on points.

"...and still Champion"

Frazier was a modest family man, a "good" champion that even prejudiced fans could admire. The sassy, colorful Muhammad Ali slipped out of the limelight, except for one moment of glory when the Supreme Court reversed his conviction for draft evasion.

In January, 1973, Joe Frazier met Olympic gold medalist George Foreman at a match in Jamaica. Foreman scored a great upset by KO'ing the champ in the 2nd round. Another clean-cut black man became heavyweight champion of the world.

Muhammad Ali was not idle during all this time. He fought and almost always won. His fists and his mouth were in fighting trim when he met the deposed Joe Frazier in a rematch and won a unanimous 12-round decision. "Now bring on George Foreman!" crowed Ali.

"My ambition is to retire Ali's mouth," replied the champion.

The great meeting was arranged in the fall of 1974. It would take place in the black African nation of Zaire, formerly Belgian Congo. The boxers would receive the largest purses in history — $5 million each. The fight would be televised *via* satellite to over a billion viewers.

Joe Frazier falls victim to Muhammad Ali's right.

The odds were 3 to 1 against Ali, who was now 32 years old to Foreman's 24. To all who would listen, Ali proclamied, "I am the greatest!" But even those who admired his spirit and respected his sincerity felt he had only a small chance against young Foreman.

On October 30,1974, Muhammad Ali and George Foreman entered the ring in Kinshasa, Zaire. The crowd was on Ali's side. Yet as the first round began, their cheers turned to gasps of dismay. Ali, the footwork specialist, the dancer, let Foreman drive him to the ropes!

Where was the floating butterfly? Where was the stinging bee? Ali's handlers pleaded for him to dance. "I know what I'm doing," he growled.

Ali let Foreman flail away. The challenger ducked Foreman's blows or absorbed them on his iron-hard muscles. The champion, winner of 40 bouts, was used to having his foes fall in the early rounds. But Ali refused to topple. Instead, he peppered the champion's face with blows. Previously, the slugging Foreman had rarely been hurt. He began to slow. All the while, Muhammad Ali spoke to Foreman, taunting him, jeering at his fighting style. "You're getting tired, George," Ali said. And it was true.

Young George Foreman wilts under the attack of Ali during their bout in Zaire, Africa.

Craftily, Ali forced Foreman to keep working. In the 8th round, Ali switched from defense to offense and waded in for the kill. He sprang off the ropes and walloped Foreman mercilessly. A hard left hook! A crushing right! George Foreman toppled to the canvas.

The referee counted, and the champion stirred. He tried to rise, then slumped back. The count ended. Muhammad Ali had regained his heavyweight title.

"I told you I was the greatest," he said. This time, the entire world agreed.

The valient comeback of Ali made sports fans forget his boastful manner, his Black Muslim ties, his controversial politics. Here was a boxer! Here was a heavyweight champ who had proved himself under the toughest conditions.

He met other opponents in the months that followed, but the verdict of the referees was always the same.

"The winner – and still heavyweight champion of the world – Muhammad Ali."

He really was the greatest, maybe the greatest ever.

Foreman falls in the 8th round as underdog Muhammad Ali regains the heavyweight championship of the world.

EVERLAST

OHAMMAD ALI
INING CAMP
LAKE, P

Heavyweight Champions of the World

Champion	Opponent	Date of Bout
John L. Sullivan	Paddy Ryan	Feb. 7, 1882
James J. Corbett	John L. Sullivan	Sept. 7, 1892
Bob Fitzsimmons	James J. Corbett	Mar. 17, 1897
James J. Jeffries*	Bob Fitzsimmons	Jun. 9, 1899
Marvin Hart	Jack Root	Jul. 3, 1905
Tommy Burns	Marvin Hart	Feb. 23, 1906
Jack Johnson	Tommy Burns	Dec. 26, 1908
Jess Willard	Jack Johnson	Apr. 5, 1915
Jack Dempsey	Jess Willard	July 4, 1919
Gene Tunney*	Jack Dempsey	Sept. 23, 1926
Max Schmeling	Jack Sharkey	Jun. 12, 1930
Jack Sharkey	Max Schmeling	Jun. 21, 1932
Primo Carnera	Jack Sharkey	Jun. 29, 1933
Max Baer	Primo Carnera	Jun. 14, 1934
James J. Braddock	Max Baer	Jun. 13, 1935
Joe Louis*	James J. Braddock	Jun. 22, 1937
Ezzard Charles	Jersey Joe Walcott	Jun. 22, 1949
Jersey Joe Walcott	Ezzard Charles	Jul. 18, 1951
Rocky Marciano*	Jersey Joe Walcott	Sept. 23, 1952
Floyd Patterson	Archie Moore	Nov. 30, 1956
Ingemar Johansson	Floyd Patterson	Jun. 26, 1959
Floyd Patterson	Ingemar Johansson	Jun. 20, 1960
Sonny Liston	Floyd Patterson	Sept. 25, 1962
Cassius Clay (Ali)**	Sonny Liston	Feb. 25, 1964
Joe Frazier***	Buster Mathis	Mar. 4, 1968
Jimmy Ellis****	Jerry Quarry	Apr. 27, 1968
Joe Frazier	Jimmy Ellis	Feb. 16, 1970
George Foreman	Joe Frazier	Jan. 22, 1973
Muhammad Ali	George Foreman	Oct. 30, 1974

*Retired undefeated
**Deposed by WBA
***Recognized in 6 states, Mexico, South America
****Recognized by World Boxing Association after elimination tournament

The most controversial heavyweight champion
proclaims to the world, "I am king!"

SPORTS CLASSICS

WORLD SERIES
U.S. OPEN GOLF CHAMPIONSHIP
WIMBLEDON TENNIS TOURNAMENT
KENTUCKY DERBY
INDIANAPOLIS 500
OLYMPIC GAMES
SUPER BOWL
MASTERS TOURNAMENT OF GOLF
STANLEY CUP
NBA PLAY-OFFS
ROSE BOWL
AMERICA'S CUP YACHT RACE
WINTER OLYMPICS
PGA CHAMPIONSHIP TOURNAMENT
TRIPLE CROWN
AMERICAN TENNIS CHAMPIONSHIP
DAYTONA 500
GRAND PRIX
BOXING'S HEAVYWEIGHT CHAMPIONSHIP

CREATIVE EDUCATION